What Do I Do When...

I'M SAD!

Danielle Haynes

PowerKiDS press

PK Beginners

I’m sad. I want to cry.

My best friend moved away. I miss her so much!

I want to yell and be mean to others.

Being sad makes me want to go to sleep.

It's hard to share my feelings when I'm sad.

Mom says everyone feels sad sometimes. It's OK.

Dad says talking to someone will help me feel better.

Mom says crying is OK. It helps get my sadness out.

We play outside.
It helps me feel better!

Mom says we can visit my friend. That makes me happy!

Feeling sad is OK. But now I know how to be happy!

Published in 2026 by The Rosen Publishing Group, Inc.
2544 Clinton Street, Buffalo, NY 14224

First Edition

Editor: Danielle Haynes
Book Design: Jeffrey Taylor

Photo Credits: Cover Luis Molinero/Shutterstock.com; p. 3 PeopleImages.com - Yuri A/Shutterstock.com; pp. 5, 13, 21 szefei/ Shutterstock.com; p. 7 Dean Drobot/ Shutterstock.com; p. 9 Anatoliy Karlyuk/Shutterstock.com; pp. 11, 15, 17 fizkes/Shutterstock.com; p. 19 sutadimages/Shutterstock.com; p. 23 Miljan Zivkovic/Shutterstock.com.

Cataloging-in-Publication Data
Names: Haynes, Danielle.
Title: I'm sad! / Danielle Haynes.
Description: Buffalo, New York : PowerKids Press, 2026. | Series: What do I do when...
Identifiers: ISBN 9781499455953 (pbk.) | ISBN 9781499455960 (library bound) | ISBN 9781499455977 (ebook)
Subjects: LCSH: Sadness in children--Juvenile literature. | Sadness--Juvenile literature. | Emotions in children--Juvenile literature.
Classification: LCC BF723.S15 H39 2026 | DDC 155.4124--dc23

Manufactured in China